— HOW TO —
CONTROL YOUR
EMOTIONS

A Practical Guide to Manage
Stressful Situations, Better
Manage Your Feelings, and
Overcome Negative
Thinking.

*Includes 7 Simple Emotion
Coping Hacks*

BARBARA S. RAINWATER

HOW TO CONTROL
YOUR EMOTIONS

A Practical Guide to Manage Stressful Situations, Better Manage Your Feelings, and Overcome Negative Thinking

Includes 7 Simple Emotion Coping Hacks

BY

Barbara S. Rainwater

Disclaimer

The Publisher has strived to be as accurate and complete as possible in the creation of this report, although she does not warrant or represent at any time that the contents within are accurate due to the rapidly changing nature of things.

While all attempts have been made to verify the information provided in this publication, the Publisher assumes no responsibility for errors, omissions, or contrary interpretations of the subject matter herein. Any perceived slights of specific persons, peoples, or organizations are unintentional.

In practical advice books, like anything else in life, there are no guarantees. Readers are cautioned to reply on their judgment about their circumstances to act accordingly.

Take everything I say in this book as my opinion and regard it as entertainment.

You are responsible for your actions by acting on the thought and views shared in this book.

You are encouraged to print this book for easy reading.

TABLE OF CONTENTS

Why This Book?

People express themselves with varying intensities of emotion every day. Some people are consistently more emotional than others. Some are even a little uptight about it, and that's okay too.

If you're reading this, I assume you have the capacity for logical thought and a willingness to understand new information about the world around you. I also assume you have the ability to successfully read this book and retain its contents. If either or both of these assumptions is incorrect, please stop reading immediately and explore other interests instead.

Continuing to read this book indicates that you are willing to learn more about the world around you as well as your own internal thoughts and processes. It also indicates that you enjoy learning new things about yourself and what makes you tick on a deeper level than just everyday conversation can provide. This information is rather personal; we don't want word getting out that we let anyone in on this little secret!

While there are many books on the topic of emotional intelligence, this book was written with a specific audience in mind: people who struggle with their emotions and who have trouble controlling them. If you find it hard to recognize when you're feeling stressed or overwhelmed, if you have a hard time identifying what you're feeling, or if you feel out of control with your emotions, this book is for you. If you want to improve your emotional intelligence, but you aren't sure where to start, this book is for you. If you want to take control of your emotions and end the vicious cycle of stress and overwhelm, this book is for you.

Introduction

Do you ever feel like your emotions are out of control? You are not alone. Many people struggle to manage their emotions in daily life. Even if you have a solid grasp of your emotions most of the time, it can be difficult to manage them during other instances.

Recognizing your emotions and responding appropriately are keys to emotional intelligence. You can't effectively deal with challenges in your life if you can't recognize when you're feeling stressed, anxious, or sad. The ability to manage your emotions also plays a big part in your ability to succeed at work, school, and home.

But how do you know if your emotions are out of control? Are there any telltale signs that indicate when you should take action and take a step back from whatever is stressing you out? Are there ways to control your emotions so they don't get the best of you? If so, what are those ways? *Yes, I allow people to affect my Emotions both good & bad*

Fortunately, developing emotional intelligence is something that can be learned and practiced over time. Everyone struggles with their emotions at some point in their lives. The good news is that it is possible to learn how to control your emotions and respond to difficult situations in a more productive way.

This book is about how to control you Emotions. In this book, you will learn about why you have emotions, what triggers them, and some coping skills to use when dealing with the emotions. Learn what it means to be emotional intelligent and the simple skills necessary for managing your moods and relationships more effectively.

SECTION ONE

Managing Your Emotions

When it comes to managing your emotions, timing is everything. If you feel stressed out at work, but you don't address it until you get home, the stress will fester and grow. You won't be able to manage it effectively and it will have an impact on your relationships and your health. On the other hand, if you recognize when you're feeling stressed and you take action to address the source, it won't grow into something much bigger. You will be able to use stress as a sign that you need to make a change or that you need to learn how to handle a situation differently.

If you struggle to manage your emotions, you might find that you experience stress and feel overwhelmed a lot. It's important to take action and change this. The more you stress out and let emotions take over, the less productive you will be. You might even start resenting the people in your life and have trouble connecting with loved ones.

Samanta Resents Me, she now thinks she made a mistake. I want to prove her wrong

What are Emotions?

Do you ever feel anxious or happy one day, and then the next day you feel the exact opposite? It's common to have ups and downs in your mood. But what exactly are emotions, and how are they formed?

An emotion is a response to a stimulus that has social implications. In other words, it's a reaction to something we see, smell, taste, hear, or touch.

There are many different kinds of emotions — sadness, fear, anger, joy and so on — but they all have one thing in common: They alert us to danger or motivate us to take action. A person's emotional state is determined by their reaction to stimuli in their environment. When these reactions cause a person distress or discomfort for extended periods of time, they are considered "disordered" emotions; this is when therapy can help.

What is the difference between emotions and feelings?

Emotions and feelings are often used interchangeably, but they actually have different meanings. When you feel happy, sad, angry, or afraid, you are experiencing a range of emotions. These emotions come and go, and they may be short-lived or last a long time. A feeling, on the other hand, is a more intense or negative emotion that lasts a short amount of time. For example, when you experience a sudden, unexpected death of a loved one, it is normal to feel stunned, numb, and depressed. But when these feelings last for a long time, they are classified as a disorder called depression.

What are the different types of emotions?

Emotions are the in-the-moment sensations that accompany our thoughts and perceptions. There are many different emotions, and each is highly individualized and unique to each person. Some of the different types of emotions are:

- Anger

- Depression

- Fear

- Guilt

- Joy

- Love

- Sadness

- Stress

How are emotions formed?

Emotions can be broken down into three parts: The physiological response, the mental association, and the behavioural response. When we experience something that causes a physiological response, like being around a loud, scary noise, chemicals in our brain called neurotransmitters are released. These neurotransmitters trigger an emotion such as fear. This is often how our emotions are formed when we are young and still developing: When we are around our parents and caregivers, we often see them feeling a certain way and associate that feeling with the situation. This is also why infants cry more often — they are trying to communicate their needs and emotions to their parents.

How do our emotions affect us physically?

Since emotions are very closely linked to our biology, they also have an impact on our health. Some emotions, like positive ones like joy and gratitude, can even have positive impacts on our health. These emotions help us relax, reduce stress, and lower our blood pressure.

When we are feeling anxious, depressed, or angry, however, they have the opposite effect. They cause our blood pressure to increase, can cause us to experience shortness of breath, and make us feel agitated.

- Loss of Appetite
- feel physically Sick

What happens when our emotions are disordered?

Emotions are powerful, but when they are disordered or out of control, they can have a negative impact on our lives. Emotions are closely tied to our thoughts and perceptions, so a disordered emotion may lead to distorted thinking. Sadness, for example, is a common emotion in the grieving process, and it can be helpful for our healing and growth. But, if sadness persists for long periods of time or is so intense that it interferes with your daily life and ability to function, it may be categorized as depression. One of the reasons therapy can be helpful is that it can help people recognize emotions that have been disordered and put them in a healthier perspective.

What are the symptoms of an emotional disorder?

Emotions naturally shift and change, but some can become disordered if they are felt frequently and/or for a long period of time. Some emotions to watch for include:
- Anxiety - Depression - Fear - Guilt - Shame – Sadness.

If you feel that one or more of these emotions take up too much space in your life or are too intense, that could be a sign that something is not right.

If you are experiencing one or more of these emotions on a daily basis and they are impacting your quality of life, it may be time to seek help.

How can we manage our emotions?

The key to managing emotions is first recognizing when they are disordered and then finding ways to regulate them. There are a few different ways you can manage your emotions, including:

- Journaling

- Try chatting a loved one or with a friend

- Getting outside: Exercise can help you relax and re-focus your attention

- Mindfulness practices: Mindfulness practices like meditation can help you recognize and regulate your emotions

- Self-Care: Taking care of your basic needs (eating well, getting enough sleep, etc.) can help you better regulate your emotions

- Cognitive restructuring: This is when you challenge your negative thoughts and replace them with more helpful and healthy thoughts.

Emotions Are A Natural

Emotions are a natural and a part of being human. All of us experience a wide range of emotions on a daily basis as we go about our lives. When handled appropriately and in a healthy manner, these emotions can be very helpful and enriching to our daily lives. But when emotions are felt too intensely or for too long, they may become disordered. When this happens, they can have a harmful impact on our mental health and ability to function. It is important to recognize when our emotions are disordered and take steps to manage them. This can be done through journaling, talking with a friend, getting outside, practicing mindfulness, taking care of yourself, and challenging your negative thoughts. By managing your emotions, you can reduce their impact on your mental health.

SECTION TWO

Emotional Intelligence

Emotional intelligence is the ability to identify and understand your emotions and the emotions of others, as well as have a positive impact on your relationships. Research has shown that people who are more emotionally intelligent are more successful in their careers and in their personal lives.

People who have high emotional intelligence are able to manage their emotions, respond to situations in a positive, productive way, and build effective relationships with others.

Identify what you're feeling

One of the first steps to controlling your emotions is being able to identify what you're feeling. Although this might sounds very simple, but many people struggle with this. If you have trouble identifying what emotion you're feeling, you will have a hard time dealing with it effectively. To get started, think about times when you are sure what you're feeling. What words would you use to describe what you're experiencing? It's likely that the exact words will come up again and again. Once you have a list of emotions, it will be much easier to identify what you're feeling throughout the day.

I feel Like Im chasing a Racehorse
re Running and I am Stuck in the mud

What are the triggers?

Now that you are able to identify what you're feeling, the next step is to figure out why you're feeling that way. Are the people around you triggering emotions in you? Is it something you're doing? Or is it a situation you're in?

Sometimes emotions are triggered by a specific event or situation. You might feel stressed out when you're behind on a project at work or when a loved one is away on a trip. These situations are known as "triggers" and they can cause you to feel a certain way. The best way to deal with these emotions is to identify the trigger. Once you know what is causing these emotions in you, it will be much easier to control them. There are a few ways to do this. -The first is to write down the things that trigger your emotions. If you're feeling stressed because you're behind on a project, write it down. If seeing someone you care about leave for a trip makes you sad, write it down. When you write down the things that trigger your emotions, you are actively working to control them.

Sam wants a break, ~~with~~ which sucks
But I have never had a say so for any
situation, she dictates

Why am I so emotional? Everything

While we're on the topic of why you're feeling the way you're feeling, it's also helpful to figure out why you have such strong emotions. Are you tired? Are you hungry? Do you need a break?

- Maybe you're tired and you just need to take a nap. Maybe you're hungry and you need a snack. Or perhaps you need a break from whatever is stressing you out.

- If you're stressed because you aren't getting enough sleep and you have a presentation the next day, that's something you can do something about. If you're feeling sad because you're hungry, you can take action there.

What can I do do about my feelings?

Now that you are able to identify what you're feeling and why you're feeling that way, the next step is to decide how to handle the emotions.

There are a several ways you can go about this.

- You can use what is known as the "ABC technique." With this technique, you focus on the situation at hand

and the emotions that come with it. You then ask what you want to achieve with the situation and what you want to do about the emotions that are stirring up inside of you.

- You can also choose to write out your feelings. If you have a lot going on and you can't figure out how to deal with your emotions, writing things down can help immensely.

Is there a healthier way of coping?

It's possible that the way you are dealing with your emotions isn't the best way. Maybe you have a tendency to turn to food when you are stressed or angry. Maybe you have a bad habit of isolating yourself when you are sad. Maybe you hold in your feelings and bottle things up until they become too much. If you find that your coping strategies are unhealthy or ineffective, it might be time to change things up. It can be helpful to talk to a loved one about your emotions and how you deal with them. -If you notice that you have a few unhealthy habits or that you use the same technique for every emotion, it might be helpful to talk to a therapist or a psychologist.

Practice acceptance and mindfulness

In order to be an emotionally intelligent person, you must first recognize how your feelings and actions are influenced by external factors. Developing self-awareness requires consistent practice and deliberate efforts to remain in the present moment.

Self-control often feels like a constant struggle for most people. In order to maintain control over our emotions and actions, we must adopt practices that challenge us as individuals and helps us see things from a different perspective.

Practicing acceptance and mindfulness will not only assist you with controlling your emotions but also ease the stress and anxiety that comes with daily life. In this blog post, you will learn strategies for practicing acceptance and mindfulness in order to control your emotions more effectively.

Write down the things that trigger your emotions

This is the last step in this process. Once you have identified what you're feeling and what is triggering these emotions, it can be helpful to write it down. This can help you to visually see your emotions and to actively work to take control of them. When emotions are written down, they become more concrete.

SECTION THREE

Emotion Control - 7 Simple Emotion Coping Strategies

When we find ourselves in a challenging situation, our natural reaction is to either react with anger, fear, sadness or frustration - or try to remain calm. How you respond to these situations will have a great impact on your personal growth. In fact, how you deal with stress and challenging situations can determine how successful and happy you will be in the long run.

In order to live a fulfilling life, we need to be able to cope with stress in a healthy way. Stressors are everywhere, and it's normal to feel stressed or anxious from time to time.

However, if stress begins to have a negative impact on your ability to function normally in everyday life, then you might want to consider adopting some coping strategies.

To effectively manage your emotions and cope with stressful situations, it's important to have strategies at hand that will help you keep a cool head no matter what. This section lists some helpful emotion-coping strategies that will make life easier when dealing with stress and challenging situations.

Stay in the present moment

One way to cope effectively with negative emotions is to stay in the present moment. When you are trapped in negative thoughts and emotions from the past or future, you are unable to make rational decisions in the present moment. "Being in the now" is about focusing on what is happening in this very moment. This will help you let go of any negative emotions and feelings that might be holding you back. Whenever you feel overwhelmed with negative emotions, try to stay in the present moment as much as you can. This will help you take a step back from the situation so you can see things from a more neutral perspective. Remember that whatever is happening in this moment will pass. You will get through it, no matter how challenging it might seem right now.

I just want her to work with me. Not run away

Think of the consequences

When you find yourself reacting to a stressful situation, it's important to think of the consequences that might follow. For example, if you have an upcoming presentation at work, and your mind begins to imagine all the things that could go wrong, you might start getting anxious or worried. You might think that the presentation is impossible, or that you will fail at it. This will most likely lead to you feeling overwhelmed and even depressed.

However, when you think of the consequences of these emotions and thoughts, you might realize that they are completely irrational. Thinking of the consequences will help you realize that there is nothing to be afraid of.

Consequences —
She will leave for good

worst case scenario

If you are honest with yourself, you will know that you are more than capable of doing your job well and making a great presentation! This will help you let go of any negative emotions and allow you to feel confident again so that you can take the necessary steps to get prepared for your presentation.

Connect with nature

When you are stressed out, it's a good idea to get out of the city for a while and connect with nature. Being in nature has a calming effect on the human mind and body. It helps you make a connection with the present moment and relieve any negative emotions that are holding you back. — Sam loves being outside

I love that about her

It's helpful to go on a walk in the woods, sit by a river, or visit the beach- any environment that makes you feel calm and connected. Even spending a few minutes looking at pictures of nature on your phone or computer screen is proven to have positive effects on your emotions.

You can also try meditating while surrounded by nature by going to a park or garden. This will help you relax and let go of any negative feelings that are holding you back.

Exercise regularly

Regular exercise is one of the best ways to manage your emotions and feel more in control of your life. It regulates the flow of chemicals in the brain that can help you remain calm, focused, and optimistic even in the face

I been Exercising

of adversity. It also releases endorphins that make you feel happy and increase your self-esteem. If you regularly exercise, you will find that you have more energy and are better able to cope with stress. You can try different types of physical activity, such as running, swimming, lifting weights, yoga, or even walking at a faster pace. The important thing is to find an exercise that you enjoy so that you will be more likely to stick with it.

Talk to your mentor or friend

When you are feeling stressed out or challenged by a situation in your life, it's important to talk to someone. Find someone whom you trust and feel comfortable talking to. This could be a friend, mentor, therapist, or psychologist.

Jeff is an Idiot
I'd Rather talk to Sam,
Even though most her Responses
are not good

Talking about your challenges and feelings will allow you to let go of any negative emotions you are holding on to. It will also give you a chance to get some new perspectives on the situation and consider different ways of looking at it. This can be very helpful, as often times we get trapped in our own head and don't see things objectively anymore.

Talking to someone you trust will make you feel lighter, and it will give you a sense of relief. You will feel empowered and ready to take on the next challenge in your life with confidence.

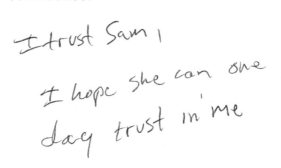

I trust Sam!
I hope she can one day trust in me

Meditate and breathe deeply

This is another great way to let go of any negative emotions and thoughts that are holding you back.

Meditation has been proven to positively affect the human body and mind. It can lower your blood pressure, reduce anxiety and depression, and increase your self-awareness and self-control.

Some people find it helpful to practice meditation with a specific goal in mind. You can try visualizing yourself in a calm place surrounded by nature. This will help you relax and let go of any negative feelings that are holding you back. You can also try focusing on your breathing for a few minutes. This will help you regulate your breathing and calm your mind down.

Write down your thoughts

When you feel like your head is full of thoughts and emotions, try writing them all down. Writing is a way of externalizing your thoughts and feelings so that you don't have to keep them bottled up inside you. It gives you a chance to explore your emotions and thoughts so that you can let go of any negative emotions that are holding you back.

You can also try writing down solutions to problems or challenges you are facing in your life. This will help you stay focused and put you in a more proactive frame of mind.

It's important to remember that you are more than capable of coping with stress and challenging situations. This is something that everyone goes through at some point in their life. It's normal, and you should not be ashamed. In fact, it's a good thing, as it shows that you are human and you are growing as a person.

The most important thing is to be patient and know that you are doing the best you can. When you feel yourself getting overwhelmed, try using one of these emotion coping strategies. They will help you feel more in control of your life and ready to take on whatever life throws at you.

SECTION FOUR

Make Your Emotions Work For You

Everyone experiences emotions on a daily basis. Our emotions also have a direct impact on our behavior. For example, if you're feeling angry, it might lead to you saying or doing things that you later regret. We all experience different kinds of emotions every day. Whether we are happy, sad, scared, excited or some other feeling, our emotions often show in the way that we behave and respond to others and situations around us. Whether it be at school, work or with friends, our emotions can sometimes get the better of us and cause problems with those around us. However, by learning how to control your emotions rather than letting them control you can go a long way in improving your relationships with others and helping you feel more confident about yourself and how you interact with others. This section explores ways you can master your emotions and make them work for you rather than against you.

I have a terrible poker face. I can not put on a fake smile I wear my Emotions

Start with a smile

A smile can change your whole outlook on a situation, so why not start your emotion control journey with a smile? Research shows that smiling can help change your brain chemistry and improve your mood. Whether you're feeling happy or sad, try smiling to see if it changes your mood and helps you feel better. You can also try smiling at others, as smiling is often seen as a friendly and welcoming gesture and can go a long way in creating a positive and friendly environment where you live, work and socialize.

Take deep breaths

When you feel stressed, anxious or angry, it's easy to get overwhelmed and in a rush to "fix" it. However, taking some time to breathe deeply can help bring you back to a place where you can think more clearly and respond to the situation in a way that is more helpful.

When you feel distressed, it's as if your body has a "fight or flight" response. Your heart rate increases, your muscles tense up, and you start to breathe more quickly and shallowly. This can be useful if you're in danger, but if you remain stressed for a long period of time, it can cause significant damage to your health.

When you take some time to breathe deeply and slowly, you can help your body return to a more relaxed state, which can help you feel better and think more clearly.

I'd love to fix Everything But some things are out of my control.

Come to understand yourself

Knowing yourself and your personality traits can go a long way in helping you understand and control your emotions. For example, if you know that you're an "introvert," then you might know that you need to be alone and have time to recharge your batteries when you start getting tired. Knowing your personality traits can also help you understand why you feel and behave in certain ways.

Depending on your personality type, you might be more prone to experiencing certain emotions, so knowing what you're prone to feeling can help you understand and respond to them better. Knowing yourself can also help you understand why you respond to certain situations in the way that you do. If you know that you're prone to feeling anxious around new people, then when you meet someone new, you can try and remind yourself that you're anxious because of your personality. Knowing why you feel the way you do can help you respond in a more helpful way.

I understand myself. I know I can be an awesome man. Ive just always been on short End of Relationships, So I am hyper vigiliant and That is my fault

See emotions as gifts

Although emotions can often feel like something that you're stuck with, they're actually gifts that help you live a fuller and richer life. There are no "bad" emotions, and all emotions have a purpose in your life. If you feel angry, then it's because you're feeling wronged and need to take action to right that wrong. If you feel anxious, then you're feeling a degree of fear and need to take action to reduce that fear. If you feel happy, then you're feeling joy and are in a place of gratitude. All these emotions have a place in your life and can help you deal with issues, solve problems, and live a more fulfilled and happy life. Understanding this can help you feel less bogged down by your emotions and more empowered by them.

I want to make memories

Deal with memories well

Memories can be both a good and bad thing. Good memories can keep you happy and give you something to smile about when you're feeling down. Bad memories, on the other hand, can seriously hinder your ability to control your emotions. When you experience a traumatic event, you might feel traumatized or re-traumatized every time the memory resurfaces. It's important to deal with these memories in a way that helps you let them go and move past them so they don't continue to negatively impact your life. There are many ways to deal with bad memories, and they may depend on the severity of the event. For example, you could try writing down the memory in a journal and then burning the journal when you're finished.

You could also try visualizing yourself at the event and then closing the door on the event, shutting it off from your everyday life.

There are many ways to deal with bad memories, but the most important thing is that you find a way that works best for you.

Cope with worry

You may find that you're prone to worrying about things that don't actually happen. This can be extremely anxiety-inducing and lead to a poor quality of life. Worrying is often accompanied by negative predictions that you're worried will come true. This can be a vicious circle that leads to constant anxiety and a feeling of being overwhelmed. The first step in coping with worry is identifying the things that trigger it. When you know what's causing the worry, you can start to take steps to reduce it. You can also try using worry dolls to take the edge off your worries.

What this entails is that you assign a worry doll to each worry and then visualize taking the worry and stuffing it into the doll. Worry dolls can be as simple as a small teddy bear, or you could go all out and buy a fancy worry doll if you want to take the visualization to the next level.

Um, worry & fear put me in this shitty situation. How I handled myself put Sam into a flight Response

Cope with fear

Fear can be a very scary and overwhelming feeling, but it's important to remember that it's often associated with an upcoming event or situation that you don't want to happen and something you can take action to prevent. Coping with fear can be a long process and may involve letting go of things in your life that you no longer want to experience fear in. It may also involve facing your fears and not running away from them. If you're experiencing fear, it can help to remind yourself that you have the power to change your situation. If you're experiencing fear at work, you can improve your situation by taking steps to learn new skills and gain more knowledge. If you're experiencing fear around your partner or in your relationship, then you can talk to your partner and explain how you're feeling.

Cope with stress and burnout

Stress is often related to work, but it can also be caused by school, family, friends, and your general lifestyle. Being busy is all well and good, but it can lead to too much on your plate and overwhelm you. This can lead to feeling stressed and burnt out. The best ways to cope with stress and avoid burnout is to be mindful of your lifestyle and how much you're taking on. It's important to set boundaries and know when to say "no" and when to ask for help. You can also try taking regular breaks from your work and other activities to allow your mind and body to rest.

I am angry ot myself. I Ruined an amazing opportunity w Samantha

Cope with anger

If you're experiencing anger, it's important to understand that it's a normal and natural emotion. However, it's also a very powerful emotion, and if you don't deal with it in the right way, it can have a significant impact on your health. Some ways to cope with anger include being around supportive people, taking some time to relax, meditate or do breathing exercises, and engaging in positive activities. It's important that you use the "three Cs" to cope with anger. The three Cs are "contain, control, and consult," and they can go a long way in helping you deal with anger.

Contain your anger by taking some time out to calm down, control your anger by recognizing that it's an emotion and you can't ignore it, and consult.

SECTION FIVE

A Formula To Reprogram Your Mind

If you are anything like me, then your mind is constantly whirring. It's buzzing with thoughts, images, memories, aspirations and processes more information in a day than we could ever fully digest. We are constantly able to control what we think about and the actions we take. However, it is when negative thoughts or emotions arise that our ability to control them becomes limited. That's because negative thoughts and emotions have an extremely strong hold on us; they hijack our minds and prevent us from thinking clearly or acting rationally. But fear not – you can reprogram your mind so that negative thoughts and emotions no longer have the same impact on you! This section post will teach you how to do just that…

I need to stay on my meds. I need to communicate effectively understand her wants/needs. Find a way to compliment her, not complicate her life

Defining Your Own Path To Happiness

Happiness is a complex emotion and one that is impossible to define as one concept. I think that one of the most important things you can do to guide your path to happiness is to be completely honest with yourself. What way do you want the life you live to look like? What do you want your future to entail? What are your dreams and aspirations? What do you plan to achieve in your life?

These are some of the questions you should be asking yourself to get to the root of what happiness means to you. What you find will be unique to you and will depend on your own experiences, desires, values and beliefs.

Sam Does!

Know What Brings You Happiness

After you have defined what happiness means to you, you need to know what brings you happiness. This can be anything from a specific feeling or activity to a person, place or object. It could be something as simple as a favorite meal or as complex as the feeling of being able to give something back to others through your work. Knowing what brings you happiness can be difficult as it can be easy to focus on what is bringing you pain or sorrow instead.

However, you have to overcome that and focus on what brings you joy. If you don't know what brings you happiness, then you will never be able to reprogram your mind to focus on that.

Make A Decision To Be Happy

This one might sound simple, but it's important. You need to decide if you want to be happy. Although this might seem obvious, it is actually a less straightforward than it might sound. Many people make the decision to be happy without ever truly believing it. With your new knowledge of what happiness means to you, you need to decide that you want to be happy no matter how you feel in the moment. This means that you have to let go of any feelings of anger, hatred or resentment.

You have to accept that you can't control everything that happens to you and that you aren't responsible for other people's actions. You have to accept that you can only control your own actions and that you have the ability to change what you don't like about your life.

Reprogram Your Mind Knowing That You Are In Control

I believe that to truly reprogram your mind, you have to truly believe that you are in control. That means that you have to accept that you have the ability to change what you don't like about your life.

You have to accept that you have the ability to reprogram your mind to think of positive things and to push away negative thoughts and emotions. You have to accept that you have the power to change your life.

Conclusion

Positive thinking isn't some fluffy concept that you can choose to believe in or not, it is a real and tangible skill that anyone can learn. With practice, you can learn to overcome negative thoughts and emotions and you can reprogram your mind to focus on more positive and happy things. This will not happen overnight and it will take a lot of effort and patience, but the results are so worth it! So don't wait any longer and start learning how to reprogram your mind today!

Free Gift

Join our mailing list today and receive a copy of

"Challenge Automatic Negative Thoughts" completely

free by clicking the link below.

https://www.aoml.online/

Plus you'll be set to get updates on all our hot new

releases and offers, so you'll never miss the stories you

love.

https://www.aoml.online/

Made in the USA
Las Vegas, NV
19 June 2023

73597907R10046